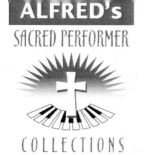

ALFRED's
SACRED PERFORMER
COLLECTIONS

What *Praise* Can I Play on Sunday?

Book 6: November and December Services

MW00813430

10 Easily Prepared Piano Arrangements

Arranged by Carol Tornquist

I have been a church pianist from a very young age, playing various styles of music from classical pieces, to hymns, to gospel songs. By the time I became involved in Christian music publishing as an arranger, praise music was emerging as the most popular musical expression of worship. Its singable melodies and catchy rhythms produced a musical style accessible to musicians and congregations alike. Today, praise songs are being sung and listened to not only on Sunday mornings but practically anytime and anywhere.

In creating this series, I have chosen the best praise songs, and they are recognizable to most congregations. Each arrangement is easy to prepare and tastefully arranged in a contemporary style appropriate for Sunday morning worship services. Book 6, for November and December, features solos for All Saints' Day, Thanksgiving, Christ the King Sunday, Advent, and Christmas. Other books in this series are as follows:

Book 1: January and February

Book 2: March and April

Book 3: May and June

Book 4: July and August

Book 5: September and October

I hope pianists will find this series to be a perfect all-in-one resource for the entire church year.

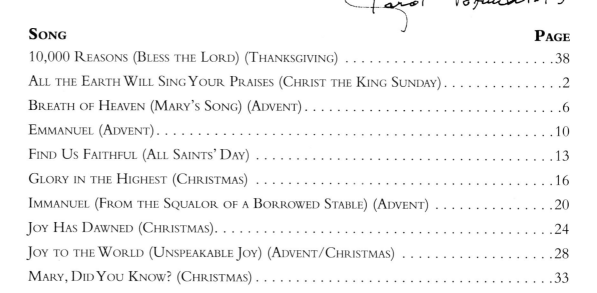

Produced by
Alfred Music
P.O. Box 10003
Van Nuys, CA 91410-0003
alfred.com

ISBN-10: 0-7390-8410-0
ISBN-13: 978-0-7390-8410-6
Cover Photo: © iStockphoto.com/mycola

2

(Approx. Performance Time – 2:30)
Christ the King Sunday

All the Earth Will Sing Your Praises

Words and Music by Paul Baloche
Arranged by Carol Tornquist

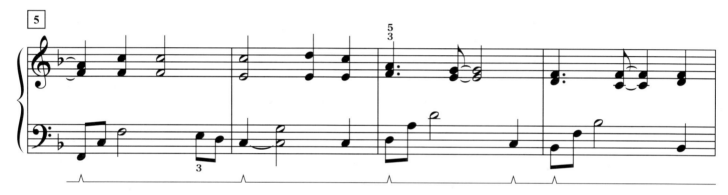

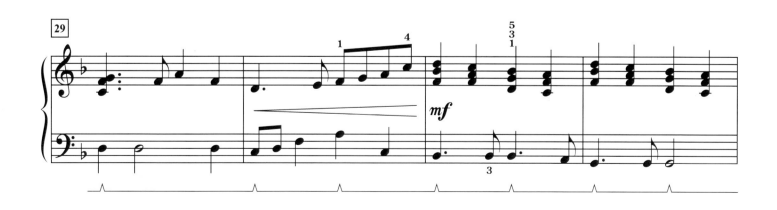

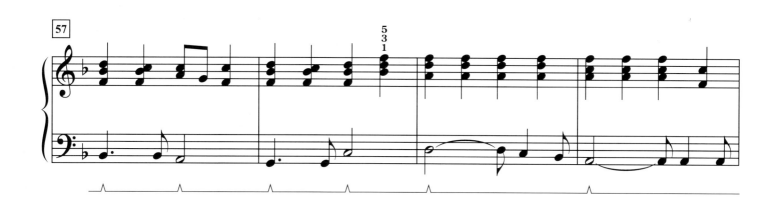

(Approx. Performance Time – 2:30)
Advent

Breath of Heaven (Mary's Song)

Words and Music by Amy Grant and Chris Eaton
Arranged by Carol Tornquist

(Approx. Performance Time – 2:00)
Advent

Emmanuel

Words and Music by Bob McGee
Arranged by Carol Tornquist

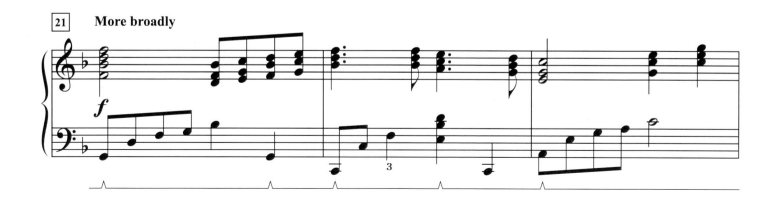

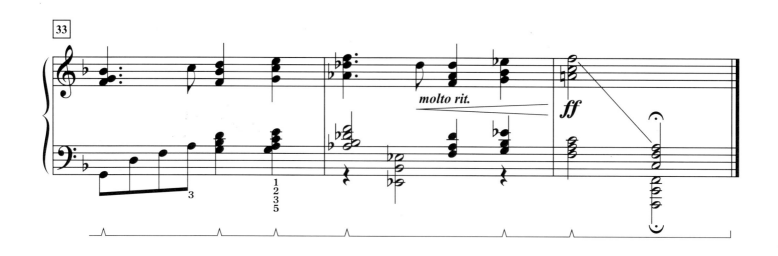

(Approx. Performance Time – 2:00)
All Saints' Day

13

Find Us Faithful

Words and Music by Jon Mohr
Arranged by Carol Tornquist

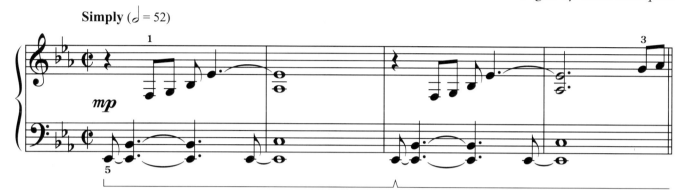

(Approx. Performance Time – 2:00)
Christmas

Glory in the Highest

Words and Music by Ed Cash, Chris Tomlin,
Jesse Reeves, Daniel Carson and Matt Redman
Arranged by Carol Tornquist

Moderately, with energy ($\bullet$ = ca. 100)

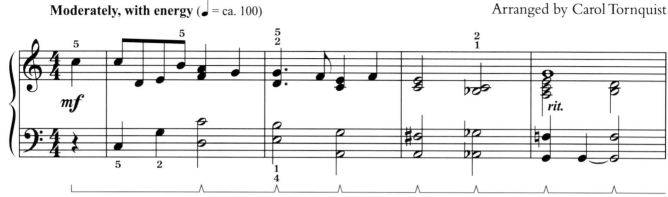

(Approx. Performance Time – 2:15)
Advent

Immanuel
(From the Squalor of a Borrowed Stable)

Words and Music by Stuart Townend
Arranged by Carol Tornquist

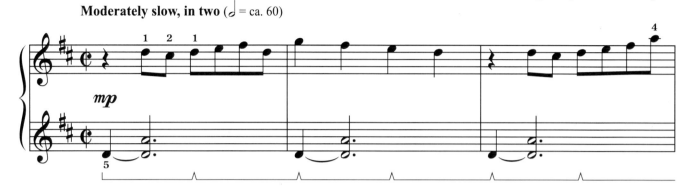

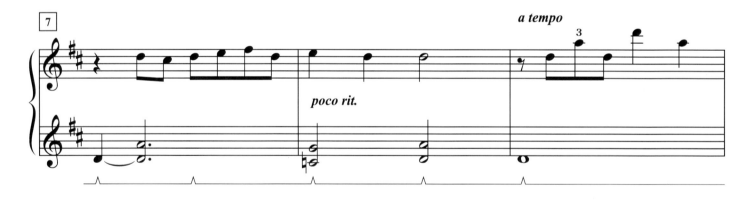

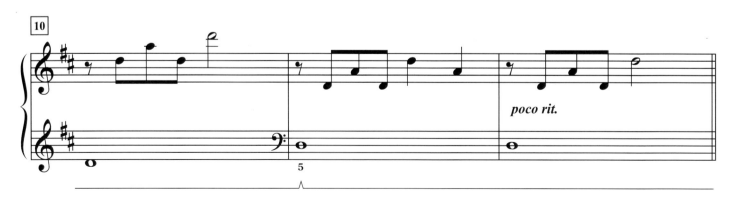

(Approx. Performance Time – 2:45)
Christmas

Joy Has Dawned

Words and Music by Keith Getty and Stuart Townend
Arranged by Carol Tornquist

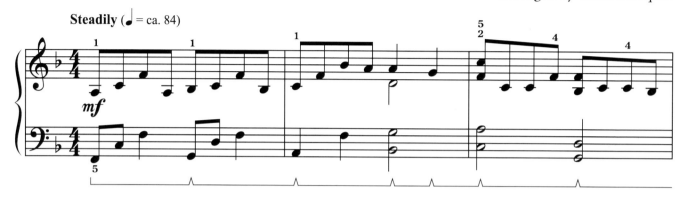

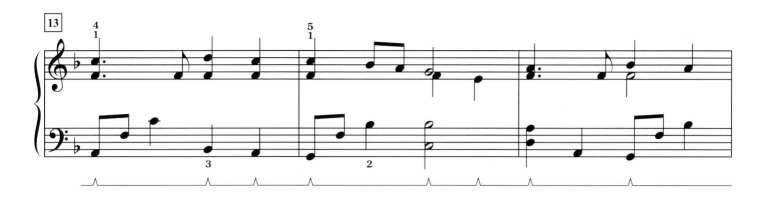

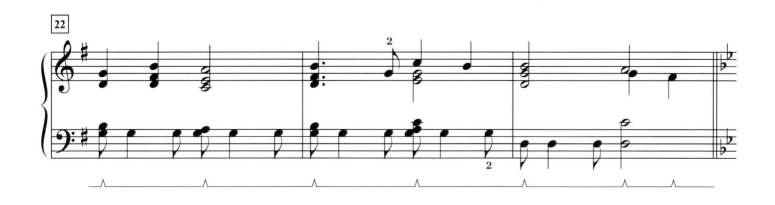

(Approx. Performance Time – 2:45)
Advent/Christmas

Joy to the World (Unspeakable Joy)

Arrangement and Additional Chorus by
Ed Cash, Matt Gilder and Chris Tomlin
Arranged by Carol Tornquist

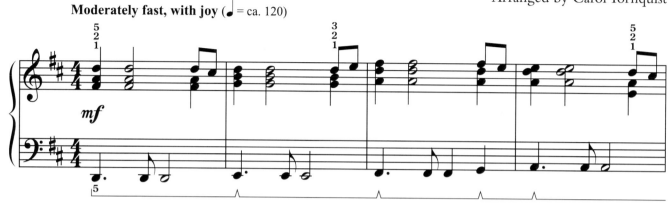

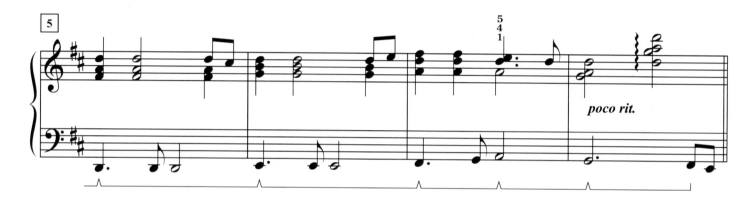

Mary, Did You Know?

Words and Music by Mark Lowry and Buddy Greene
Arranged by Carol Tornquist

(Approx. Performance Time – 2:15)
Thanksgiving

10,000 Reasons (Bless the Lord)

Words and Music by Matt Redman and Jonas Myrin
Arranged by Carol Tornquist

Simply, with reverence (♩ = ca. 72)

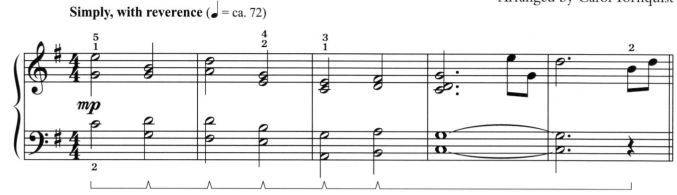

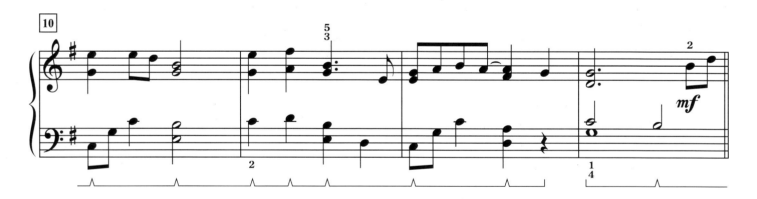